Contents

Introduction

The German Ferdinand Porsche (1875–1951) was one of the leading car engineers of the 20th century. He helped to build several early models for Mercedes and also invented the Volkswagen. He started his own company, which he ran along with his son, Ferdinand 'Ferry' Porsche, Jr. (1909–1998). In 1948 they produced the first sports car bearing the Porsche name. Porsche became known as one of the top

The Porsche badge includes symbols linked to Stuttgart, the city where Porsche is based.

The 944 Turbo reflected Porsche's priorities. Its huge 2.5-litre engine provided great speed but poor fuel efficiency.

CJJ

CARS

PORSCHE

2011
1

Lee Stacy

This paperback edition
first published in 2007 by
Franklin Watts
338 Euston Road
London NW1 3BH

Franklin Watts Australia
Hachette Children's Books
Level 17/207 Kent Street
Sydney NSW 2000

ISBN 978 0 7496 7247 8

A CIP catalogue record for this book is available
from the British Library

Printed in China

For The Brown Reference Group plc

Editor: Bridget Giles
Managing Editor: Tim Cooke
Design Manager: Lynne Ross
Children's Publisher: Anne O'Daly
Production Director: Alastair Gourlay
Editorial Director: Lindsey Lowe

Credits
Pictures: IMP AB
Text: The Brown Reference Group plc/
IMP AB

Some words are shown in **bold**, like this.
You can find out what they mean by looking
at the bottom right of most right-hand pages.
You can also find most of the words in the
Glossary on page 30.

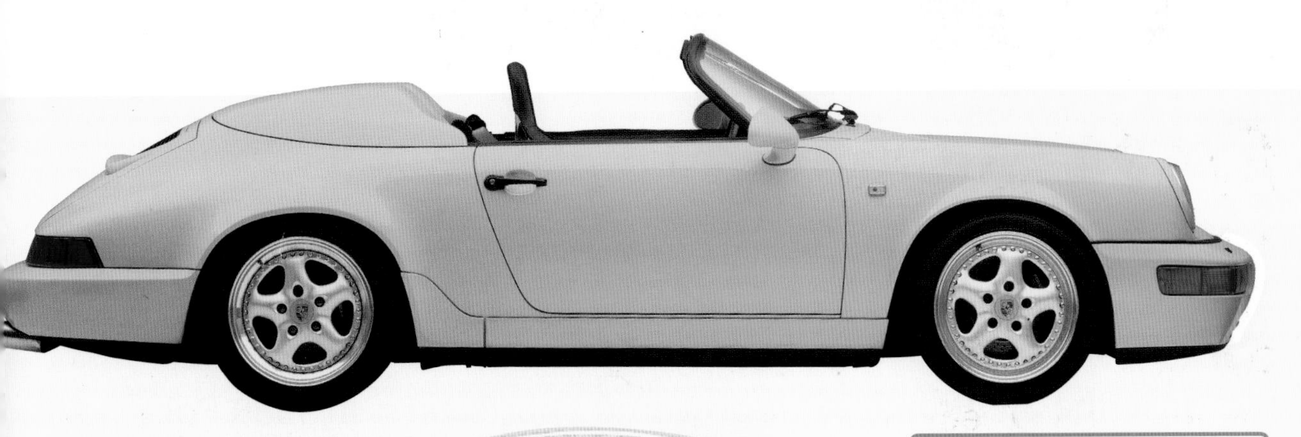

manufacturers of racing and sports cars. Today the name Porsche stands for speed, high quality and success. Porsche cars are expensive, but they give drivers unrivalled performance. Some of the most important Porsches of recent years include the limited-edition 924 Carrera, the famous 959, the 944 Turbo, the 911 Speedster, the 968 and the highly popular Boxster.

The 911 Speedster combines 1950s style with late 1980s technology. Able to reach nearly 242 km/h (150 mph), it is a car fan's dream.

The Porsche Boxster is one of the best-selling sports cars of the past 50 years. Its design is based on an earlier Porsche classic, the 550 Spyder of the 1950s.

Porsche 924 Carrera GT

Since the mid-1950s Porsche has used the term 'Carrera' to describe all of their high-powered sports cars. In 1980 Porsche created a sports car to run in the 24-hour endurance race at Le Mans, France. The company named the new model the 924 Carrera. The car did well on the race track, so Porsche made a limited edition of 400 vehicles. Today they are highly valued by collectors.

Vital Statistics for the 1980 Porsche 924 Carrera GT	
Top speed:	*240 km/h (149 mph)*
0–60 mph:	*6.5 seconds*
Engine:	*In-line four*
Engine size:	*1,984 cc (121.1 ci)*
Power:	*210 bhp at 6,000 rpm*
Weight:	*1,180 kg (2,602 lb)*
Fuel economy:	*18 mpg*

The seats are low in the limited-edition 924 Carrera because it is really more of a racing car than a road car.

Milestones

1976

The 924 becomes Porsche's new affordable model, with a front-mounted engine.

1979

Porsche increases the engine power from 125 bhp to 170 bhp in the 924 Turbo. It is Porsche's best-selling car.

1980

Porsche creates the limited-edition 924 Carrera GT, originally as a Le Mans race car. Although based on the 924 Turbo, it has a far more powerful engine. Only 400 are made.

"The 924 Carrera GT's roadholding is unbeatable and its high-speed stability is outstanding. The stiffened suspension gives a flat and firm ride at high speed."

*Even the **turbocharged** 924 Carrera is outpaced by the 924 Carrera GTR, which has a top speed of 290 km/h (180 mph). The GTR engine has an output of 375 bhp at 6,400 rpm.*

Turbocharged A word describing an engine that uses compressed air to burn fuel, giving more power.

Specifications

The design of the 924 Carrera influenced later generations of Porsches. It had wider tyres than earlier Porsches, for example. It needed wider mudguards to cover them. The same feature also occurred on the Porsche 944.

Adapted turbo engine

The engine in the 924 Carrera is based on an Audi-Volkswagen 2 litre. In the 924 Carrera, however, the turbocharged engine can produce 210 bhp, over twice as much as the engine's original 95 bhp.

Pop-up headlights

The 924 Carrera has pop-up headlights, which were fashionable in the early 1980s. When raised, the headlights disrupt the smooth flow of air over the car.

To give perfect balance between the front and rear of the 924 Carrera, the five-speed **transmission** is mounted in the rear of the car. It offsets the weight of the front-end engine.

The rear **suspension** uses a system of bars instead of coil springs to absorb bumps while keeping the car low.

Racing wheels

Like most Le Mans racing cars, the 924 Carrera has extra-wide tyres to grip the road better at high speeds. To cover the tyres, Porsche designed wide mudguards.

PORSCHE 924 CARRERA GT

Bonnet vent

The small vent or intake in the bonnet draws in air that helps to cool the turbocharger.

arge rear window

'he lid of the boot is also the ar's rear window. The glass in he rear window is a large, single ane that raises manually.

Suspension A system of springs that support a car and make it travel more smoothly.

Transmission The speed-changing gears that transmit power from the engine to the axles.

Porsche 959

The Porsche 959 is a supercar—at a super price. It cost around £325,000 when it was first made in the mid-1980s. The price was matched by the car's performance. It won both the Le Mans 24-hour race and the Paris-Dakar Rally. With its top speed of 306 km/h (190 mph), the Porsche 959 is clearly one of the top sports cars of all time. It far outperforms its nearest rivals, the Ferrari Testarossa and the Lamborghini Countach.

Vital Statistics for the 1987 Porsche 959	
Top speed:	*306 km/h (190 mph)*
0–60 mph:	*3.7 seconds*
Engine:	*Flat-six*
Engine size:	*2,851 cc (174 ci)*
Power:	*450 bhp at 6,500 rpm*
Weight:	*1,451 kg (3,199 lb)*
Fuel economy:	*13 mpg*

Unlike the 924 Carrera, the 959 has a comfortable cockpit that includes leather seats and some electrical gadgets. Even so, the model is still more of racer than a ***road car****.*

Milestones

1989

Porsche introduces the 959 at the Frankfurt Motor Show. It is both a supercar for the road and a Group B racer.

1984

The racing version starts well on the race circuit, winning the highly competitive Paris–Dakar Rally.

1987

Porsche begins production of the street-legal 959. Only 250 cars are made, some with air conditioning and leather seats, some more sporty. Each car sells for around £325,000.

"It's obvious why this is one of the most desired cars in recent history. At 4,500 rpm civilized turns to savage and you're howling past 97 km/h (60 mph) in four seconds."

The Porsche 959 had an amazing year on the racing circuit in 1986. Top race-car drivers René Metge and Jacky Ickx finished first and second, respectively, in the Paris–Dakar Rally. The rally is considered the toughest off-road race in the world.

Road car A car designed for driving on normal roads.

Specifications

The design of the 959 is based on the original Porsche 911. The car company wanted to remind car fans of the ***aerodynamic*** *shape of the 911, one of the most popular sports cars of the 1960s. The stylish shape has rarely been bettered.*

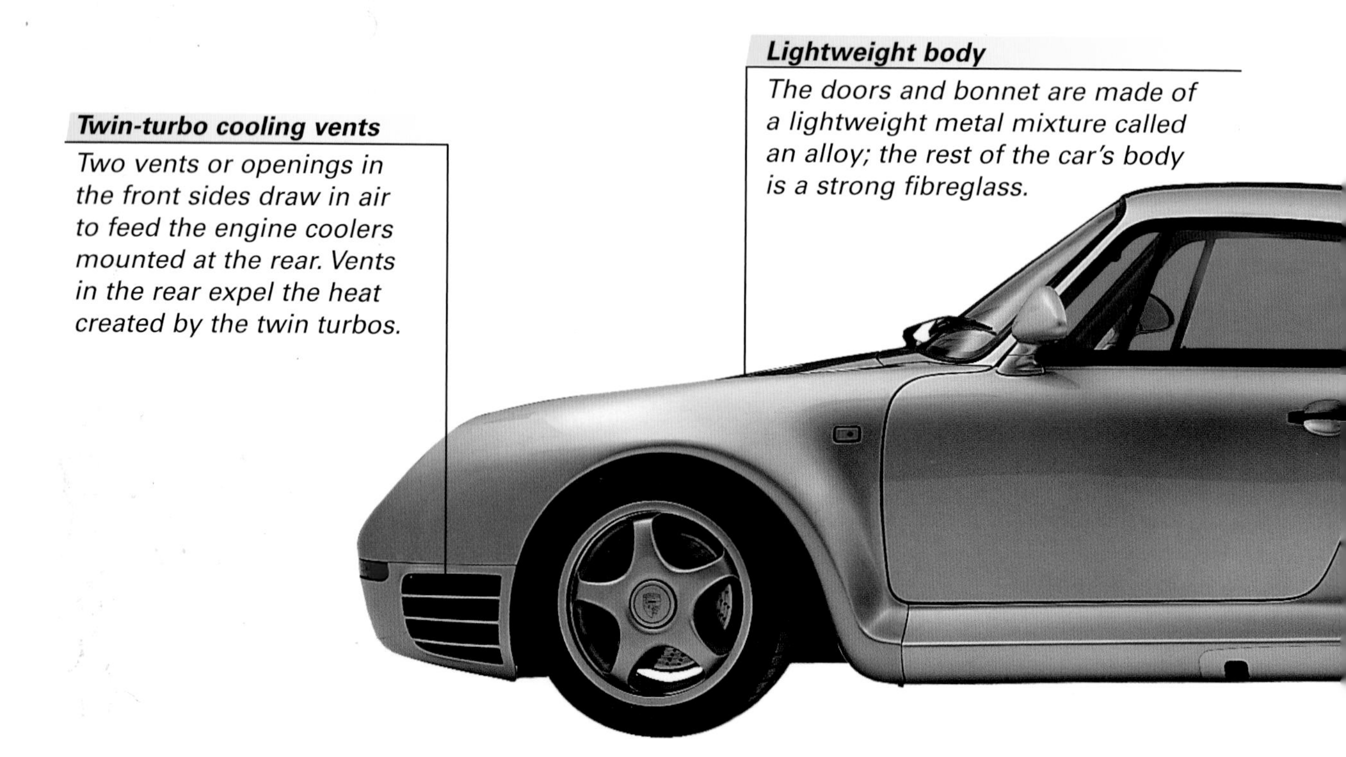

Twin-turbo cooling vents

Two vents or openings in the front sides draw in air to feed the engine coolers mounted at the rear. Vents in the rear expel the heat created by the twin turbos.

Lightweight body

The doors and bonnet are made of a lightweight metal mixture called an alloy; the rest of the car's body is a strong fibreglass.

The Porsche 959 has eight shock absorbers, devices in the suspension that help the car ride smoothly. The shocks are adjustable to match the condition of the road.

The engine has two turbochargers for extra power. One operates up to 4,000 rpm, and when the second one kicks in it helps the engine to create an extra 150 bhp.

Ultimate control

For complete control, the 959 has ***four-wheel drive*** *and a six-speed transmission.*

Long, wide mudguards

To protect the especially large front and rear tyres, the mudguards are arched long and wide over each wheel.

Special rear spoiler

The rear spoiler (or aerofoil) is large. Air pushes down on the spoiler to keep the rear tyres pressed tight to the road even at high speeds.

Aerodynamic	Designed to pass smoothly through the air.
Four-wheel drive	A system in which the engine powers all four wheels.

Porsche 944 Turbo

During the late 1980s the 944 Turbo was considered one of Porsche's most enjoyable cars to drive. From the turbocharged engine to the aerodynamic front bumper, the model was designed for power and speed. Able to reach a top speed of 248 km/h (154 mph), the Porsche 944 Turbo was stiff competition for both the Nissan 300 Zx Turbo and the Ferrari 348. The sacrifice for the power, however, was poor **fuel economy**, with less than 16 mpg.

Vital Statistics for the 1991 Porsche 944 Turbo	
Top speed:	*248 km/h (154 mph)*
0–60 mph:	*5.9 seconds*
Engine:	*In-line four*
Engine size:	*2,479 cc (153.3 ci)*
Power:	*247 bhp at 6,000 rpm*
Weight:	*1,350 kg (2,977 lb)*
Fuel economy:	*15.7 mpg*

The sleek, dark wraparound fascia has large air vents that control the temperature inside the car.

Milestones

1981

The design for the Porsche 944 Turbo is unveiled. Plans for production begin.

1985

After four years of problems, including a strike by some of the workers, Porsche finally launches the 944 Turbo.

1988

Porsche gives the 944 Turbo a larger turbocharger. This increases the power from 220 bhp to 247 bhp.

1992

The 944 Turbo is replaced by the Porsche 968.

"Balanced weight distribution and wide rear tyres equal excellent ***traction.*** *The 944 Turbo readily puts all its power onto the road and rockets off the line."*

In 1991 Porsche made a soft-top version of the 944 Turbo. The convertible was as powerful as the hardtop. Although it was well received, production only lasted for a little over one year.

Fuel economy	How many miles a car can travel on a gallon of petrol.
Traction	The grip between a tyre and the surface of the road.

Specifications

Many features of the 944 Turbo make the model special. For instance, the engine has a specially designed turbocharger that creates greater power, and the five-speed transmission is mounted in the rear to give better weight balance.

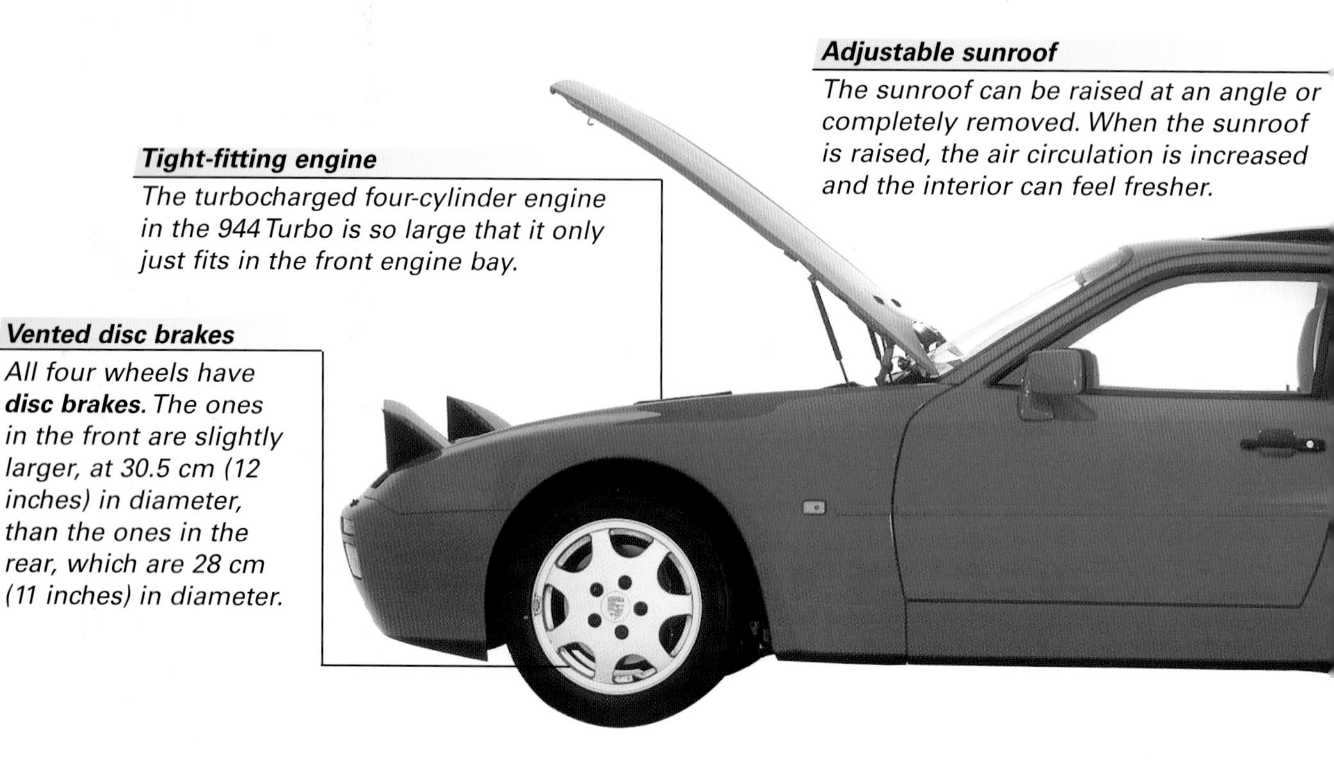

Adjustable sunroof

The sunroof can be raised at an angle or completely removed. When the sunroof is raised, the air circulation is increased and the interior can feel fresher.

Tight-fitting engine

The turbocharged four-cylinder engine in the 944 Turbo is so large that it only just fits in the front engine bay.

Vented disc brakes

All four wheels have **disc brakes.** *The ones in the front are slightly larger, at 30.5 cm (12 inches) in diameter, than the ones in the rear, which are 28 cm (11 inches) in diameter.*

Because compressed air is hot, part of the turbocharger system, called the intercooler, cools the compressed air before the air enters the engine's cylinder.

The exhaust gases produced by burning fuel leave the engine via a catalytic converter, which takes out pollutants. The cleaned exhaust then passes through the **silencer**.

Aerodynamic mudguards

The 944 Turbo has flared mudguards just like earlie Porsches. The guards help to protect the wide tyres and improve the car's overall aerodynamics.

Rear-mounted transmission

The five-speed transmission is towards the rear of the car, giving even weight distribution. When the front and rear of a car balance, it handles better.

Spacious storage area

The 944 Turbo has an exceptionally large space for storing luggage. This makes it a practical car for travelling, even though nearly everything else about the car makes it better suited to racing than road travel.

Disc brakes A type of brake with a rotating disc inside the wheel mechanism. A clip pinches the discs to stop the wheels.

Silencer A part of the exhaust system that reduces noise.

Porsche 911 Speedster

The limited-edition 911 Speedster is a **convertible** with a low windscreen, giving riders the ultimate wind-through-the-hair experience. The design is based on the 356 Speedster of the 1950s. Under the bonnet, however, the new Speedster uses the powerful 911 Carrera engine to achieve a top speed of 240 km/h (149 mph). The car is a true collectors' model: Porsche made fewer than 1,700.

Vital Statistics for the 1989 Porsche 911 Speedster	
Top speed:	*240 km/h (149 mph)*
0–60 mph:	*6 seconds*
Engine:	*Six-cylinder*
Engine size:	*3,164 cc (193.1 ci)*
Power:	*214 bhp at 5,900 rpm*
Weight:	*1,327 kg (2,925 lb)*
Fuel economy:	*24 mpg*

The two-tone, no frills interior of the 911 Speedster has gauges that are easy to read. The gear stick and steering wheel are perfectly positioned.

Milestones

1987

The prototype of the 911 Speedster is featured by Porsche at the international motor show in Frankfurt. The design is based on Porsche's 356 Speedster of the 1950s.

1989

The 911 Speedster goes into production, but Porsche chooses to make fewer than 1,700 of them. They sell for nearly £110,000 each.

1998

Ten years later, the 911 Speedster is a valuable collectors' item.

"Any Porsche 911 is a unique driving experience, but the Speedster feels special. The flat-six engine rockets you down the road."

Driving with the soft top down is the best way to experience the 911 Speedster. It is not the fastest 911 model, but the driving experience makes it a firm favourite.

Convertible A type of car that has a top that can be lowered or removed.

Specifications

From every angle, the Porsche 911 Speedster looks like a classic. Collectors value it because it is a rare car. They also appreciate its perfect combination of a sporty body and a powerful flat-six engine.

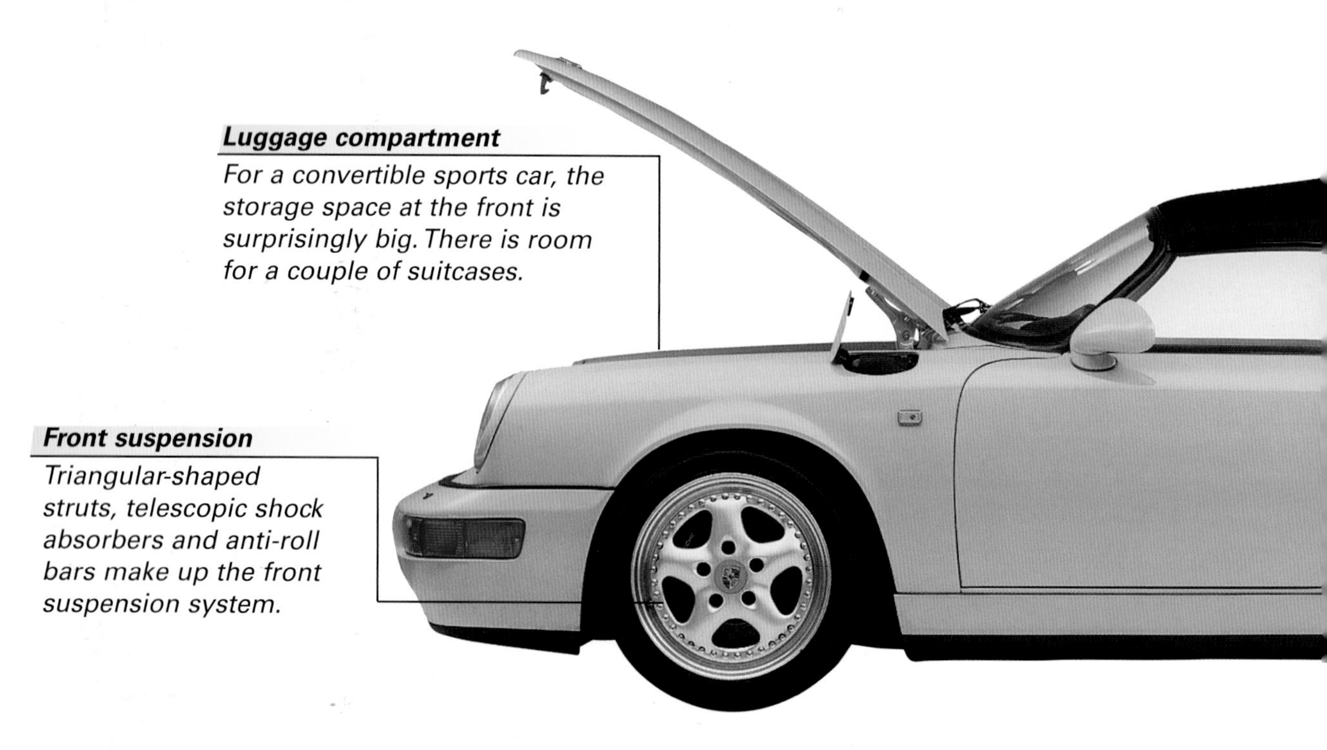

Luggage compartment

For a convertible sports car, the storage space at the front is surprisingly big. There is room for a couple of suitcases.

Front suspension

Triangular-shaped struts, telescopic shock absorbers and anti-roll bars make up the front suspension system.

The car is heavier in the back than in the front because of the rear-mounted engine. The result of this means that the driver has to take care sometimes when turning corners. Despite this, the traction of the 911 Speedster is very good.

Because the windscreen is so low, putting up the soft top does not leave much headroom in the **cockpit**.

Adjustable spoiler

The rear spoiler (or aerofoil) ca be lowered or raised. When th car is travelling at high speeds it is better to have it raised. Th raised spoiler helps to create ***downforce****, which presses the car against the road.*

Old-style headlights

The large, circular headlights are designed to look like the ones on the classic Porsches of the 1950s and 1960s.

Angled windscreen

Porsche designers made the windscreen low and steeply angled to make the 911 Speedster look similar to the 356 Speedster of the 1960s.

Cockpit	The area inside the car where the driver sits.
Downforce	A downward force created by the air pushing down on the car.

Porsche 968

Porsche introduced the 968 in the early 1990s to replace the highly popular 944. The company based the design loosely on that of the earlier Porsche 928. The new car measured up well to the 944. It was one of Porsche's easiest sports cars to drive. The front-to-rear weight balance added to the car's excellent **roadholding**. Until it was replaced by the Boxster, the 968 sold well despite its high price. The car cost between £80,000 and £100,000.

Vital Statistics for the 1995 Porsche 968 Club Sport	
Top speed:	*241 km/h (150 mph)*
0–60 mph:	*6.1 seconds*
Engine:	*In-line four*
Engine size:	*2,990 cc (182.5 ci)*
Power:	*240 bhp at 6,200 rpm*
Weight:	*1,335 kg (2,943 lb)*
Fuel economy:	*19.4 mpg*

Like other Porsches of the early 1990s, the 968 had an interior that was functional rather than luxurious.

Milestones

1979

The 924, launched in 1976, becomes a turbo, with engine power of 170 bhp.

1985

Porsche replaces the 924 Turbo with the 944 and then the 944 Turbo. The engine is larger and its power output is 220 bhp.

1991

Some changes to the 944 Turbo's body and engine transform it into the 968.

1995

Production of the 968 ends to make way for the Boxster.

"Anyone can drive the 968 well. The front-engine, rear-transaxle design gives the 968 perfect poise and balance so you can exploit all the 240 bhp from the big 3-litre four."

The Club Sport version of the 968 was lighter and slightly faster than the original. Porsche achieved this by removing the back seats and changing the front seats. The company also lowered the car and modified the tyres to give better traction.

Roadholding A car's ability to grip the road, especially at high speeds.

Specifications

The four-cylinder engine in the Porsche 968 is mounted in the front of the car. Although it does not have a turbocharger, the engine is still powerful enough to compete well against the Mazda RX-7 and the Mitsubishi 3000GT.

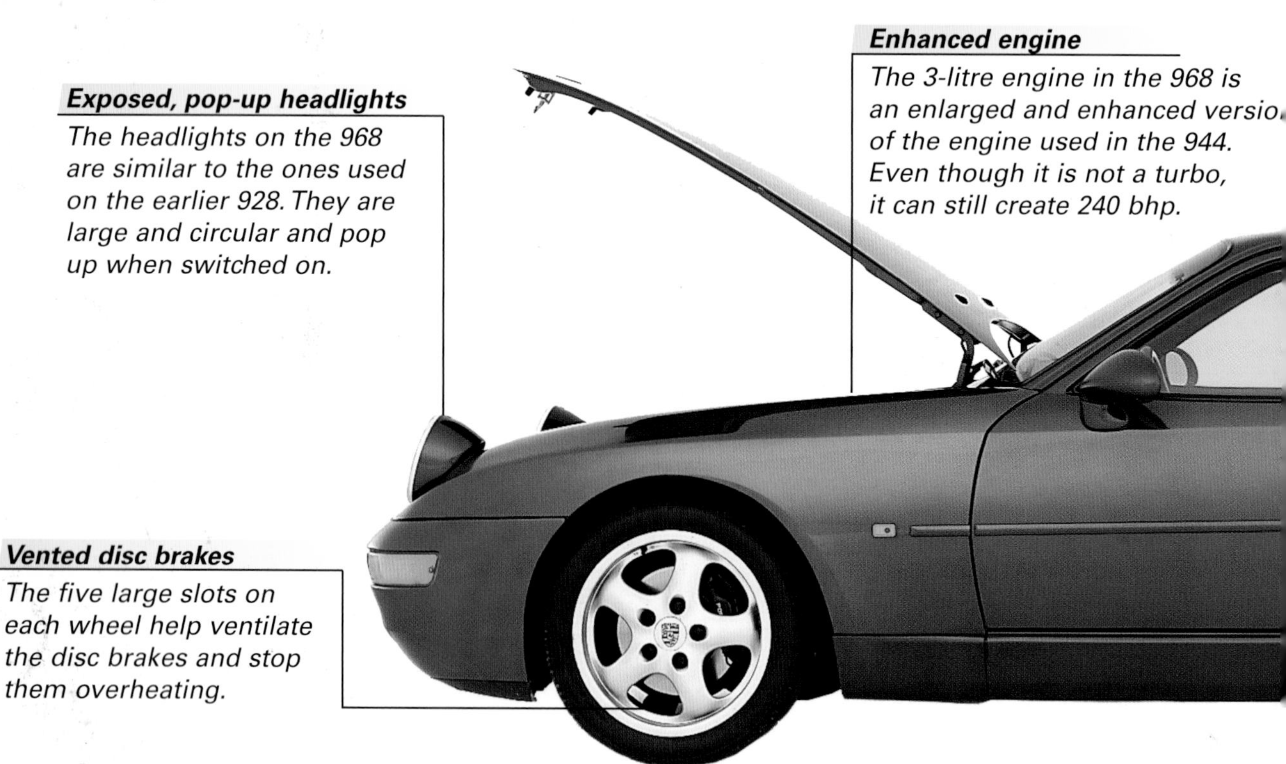

Exposed, pop-up headlights

The headlights on the 968 are similar to the ones used on the earlier 928. They are large and circular and pop up when switched on.

Enhanced engine

The 3-litre engine in the 968 is an enlarged and enhanced versio of the engine used in the 944. Even though it is not a turbo, it can still create 240 bhp.

Vented disc brakes

The five large slots on each wheel help ventilate the disc brakes and stop them overheating.

Although the 968 Club Sport had the same body and **chassis** as the more comfortable coupé, nearly all of the safety features and electronic gadgetry were stripped away to make the car as light and as fast as possible.

The Porsche 968 has the same **wheelbase**, 240 cm (94 inches), as the 944 Turbo and the 924 Carrera.

Rear spoiler, better balance

The rear spoiler (aerofoil) and the rear-mounted transmission improve handling at high speeds. The spoiler increases downforce on the car, and the weight of the transmission helps to improve overall balance.

Traditional mudguards

Like the 924 Carrera and the 944, the Porsche 968 has flared mudguards in the front and rear to cover the extra wide tyres.

Luggage area

When the rear seats in the 968 fold down, there is plenty of room in the back for large suitcases.

Chassis The supporting frame of the car on which the body is fixed.

Wheelbase The distance between the front and back axles.

Porsche Boxster

The Boxster is one of the most popular models Porsche has ever produced. Officially launched in 1996 at the Paris Motor Show, the car was praised for its excellent roadholding. It responded quickly to the driver. Innovations to the engine, such as the four overhead **camshafts**, helped to make the car powerful but still efficient. The demand for the Boxster was much higher than Porsche had expected.

Vital Statistics for the 1997 Porsche Boxster	
Top speed:	*240 km/h (149 mph)*
0–60 mph:	*6.9 seconds*
Engine:	*Flat-six*
Engine size:	*2,480 cc (151.3 ci)*
Power:	*204 bhp at 6,000 rpm*
Weight:	*1,250 kg (2,756 lb)*
Fuel economy:	*23.5 mpg*

The Boxster's instrument panel is high-tech but compact. The speedometer and other gauges overlap.

Milestones

1991

The chief designer at Porsche, Harm M. Legaay, starts work on a new sports car. He decides to base it on the 550 Spyder of the 1950s.

1993

The prototype of the Boxster is displayed at various motor shows. The design receives high praise from critics.

1996

The Boxster goes on sale. It is Porsche's first totally new model for 20 years. Porsche struggles to meet demand.

"The Boxster is still the best-handling car that Porsche has ever made. Its mid-engine design means it changes direction immediately at the touch of the incredibly precise steering."

The sleek, aerodynamic body of the Boxster has been highly praised by critics as being one of the most impressive car designs of recent times. The Boxster's innovative water-cooled flat-six engine has also received much acclaim.

Camshaft A rotating rod that opens and closes the valves in the engine. The valves let in new fuel and expel exhaust gases.

Specifications

The design of the Porsche Boxster is based on the Porsche 550 Spyder of the 1950s. The Spyder was a sporty convertible that remains a favourite among car enthusiasts. Driving either model with the top down is pure pleasure.

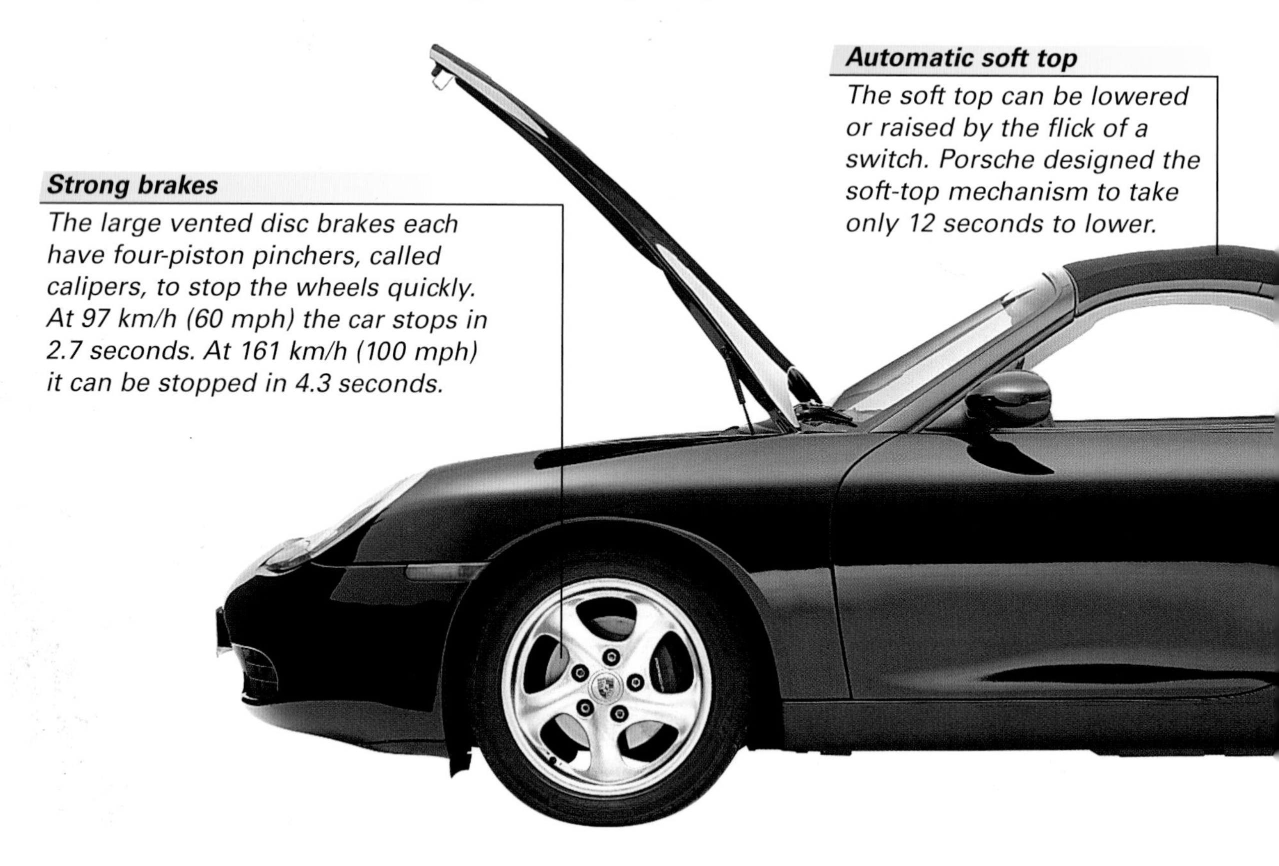

Strong brakes

The large vented disc brakes each have four-piston pinchers, called calipers, to stop the wheels quickly. At 97 km/h (60 mph) the car stops in 2.7 seconds. At 161 km/h (100 mph) it can be stopped in 4.3 seconds.

Automatic soft top

The soft top can be lowered or raised by the flick of a switch. Porsche designed the soft-top mechanism to take only 12 seconds to lower.

Most Porsches have a five-speed transmission, but the Boxster can come with a five-speed semiautomatic transmission for drivers who prefer a clutchless car.

The Porsche Boxster can outrun both the Mercedes-Benz SLK and the BMW Z3 2.8. It can also go from 0 to 97 km/h (60 mph) quicker than its competitors.

Aerodynamic underside

To improve aerodynamics, the underside of the Boxster is streamlined and high off the ground. There are also ***alloy*** *suspension arms, which help make the car as light as possible.*

r-mounted engine

water-cooled engine is ıted behind the cockpit ' is accessed by raising rear bonnet.

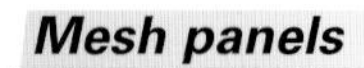

Mesh panels

The top of the windscreen frame has special mesh panels that help to protect the occupants from the wind when the soft top is down.

Alloy	A strong but lightweight metal made by mixing other metals.

Glossary

aerodynamic: *Designed to pass smoothly through the air.*

alloy: *A strong but lightweight metal made by mixing other metals.*

camshaft: *A rod that opens and closes the engine valves that let in new fuel and expel exhaust gases. It works in sync with the pistons.*

chassis: *The supporting frame of the car on which the body is fixed.*

disc brake: *A type of brake with a rotating disc inside the wheel mechanism. A clip pinches the disc to stop the wheel.*

downforce: *A downward force created by the air pushing down on the car. Rear spoilers (aerofoils) create a downforce.*

fuel economy: *How much petrol a car uses over a certain distance, such as miles per gallon.*

silencer: *A part of the exhaust system that reduces noise.*

suspension: *A system of springs that supports a car and helps it travel smoothly.*

traction: *The grip between a tyre and the surface of the road.*

transmission: *Speed-changing gears and other parts (such as the drive shaft linking gears to wheels) that transmit power from the engine to the wheels.*

turbocharger: *A device that sends compressed air into the cylinders. Compressed air leaves room for more fuel. The high level of fuel mixed with compressed air creates more power when exploded (combusted).*

Further Information

websites

http://auto.howstuffworks.com/engine.htm
How Stuff Works: Car Engines

www11.porsche.com
Porsche

www.pca.org
Porsche Club of America

books

- Adler, Dennis. ***Porsche: The Road from Zuffenhausen***. Random House, 2003.
- Frere, Paul. ***Porsche 911 Story.*** Haynes Group, 2006.
- Heilig, John. ***Sports Car Icons: Jaguar, Ferrari and Porsche.*** Motorbooks International, 2004.
- Reisser, Sylvain. ***Porsche.*** Motorbooks International, 2003.
- Vann, Peter, et al. ***Porsche Turbo: The Full History of the Race and Production Cars.*** Motorbooks International, 2000.

Index